Editor
Lorin E. Klistoff, M.A.

Managing Editor
Karen Goldfluss, M.S. Ed.

Editor-in-Chief
Sharon Coan, M.S. Ed.

Illustrator
Teacher Created Materials Staff

Cover Artist
Barb Lorseyedi

Art Coordinator
Kevin Barnes

Imaging
James Edward Grace

Product Manager
Phil Garcia

Publishers
Rachelle Cracchiolo, M.S. Ed.
Mary Dupuy Smith, M.S. Ed.

Full-Color Literacy Activities
Reading & Writing

Authors

Keri King and Kari Sickman

Teacher Created Materials, Inc.
6421 Industry Way
Westminster, CA 92683
www.teachercreated.com

ISBN-0-7439-3237-4

©2003 *Teacher Created Materials, Inc.*

Reprinted, 2004

Made in U.S.A.

Table of Contents

Introduction

Full-Color Literacy Activities: Reading & Writing includes many quick, easy, colorful, and fun literacy activities and games for you to use with your students. Whether you are a first-year teacher or a seasoned veteran, you will be overjoyed at the wealth of materials included in this book to supplement your literacy program.

This book provides a variety of unique hands-on activities and games that encourage language exploration. Students will participate in activities that focus on reading and writing. As a result, students develop literacy skills in ways that meet individual learning needs.

Each lesson defines the literacy skill and the different ways of student grouping. The lesson states clear and simple directions to allow you to quickly assemble the learning activities for your students, substitute teachers, and/or take-home activities. Most of the materials needed for the activities are included in the book. Since many of the activities are generic, they can be adapted to meet a variety of individual needs.

This book offers new and creative ideas and a fresh twist on commonly-used activities to help teachers save time and assist children in being successful literacy students.

Writing Activities

Letter Roll and Write

Literacy Skills

- writing letters A–Z
- letter identification
- letter/sound recognition

Student Grouping

- center
- small group
- independent

Materials

Each student will need the following:

- 1 copy of Letter Roll and Write Sheet (1/2 of page 6)
- dice with letters A–Z
- 1 pencil

Directions

Have each student do the following:

1. Roll a die and say the letter and sound.
2. Write that letter in a box.
3. Choose a new die and roll. Write that letter in the next box.
4. Continue to roll and write until all of the boxes are filled in.

Helpful Hints

- Have extra copies of the Letter Roll and Write Sheet available.
- Use wooden blocks to make letter dice or purchase letter dice from an educational supply store.

Letter Roll and Write Sheet

Name _____

- -

Letter Roll and Write Sheet

Name _____

Missing Letters

Literacy Skill

- writing letters alphabetically

Student Grouping

- center
- small group
- whole group
- independent

Materials

Each student will need the following:

- 1 copy of Missing Letters Sheet (page 9 or 10)
- 1 pencil

Directions

Have each student do the following:

1. Say the first letter, "a." Trace over it.
2. Write the letter that comes next—*b*.
3. Continue until all boxes have the correct letters.
4. Say the alphabet as he or she checks to make sure the letters are in alphabetical order.

Helpful Hints

- Have extra copies available.
- Laminate each sheet and have the student use letter tiles instead.

Missing Letters Sheet

Name _____

a		c			f
	h		j		
m		o			r
	t			w	
	z				

A			D		
		I		K	
	N		P		
S		U			X

Missing Letters Sheet

Name _____

a					

A					

Word Roll and Write

Literacy Skills

- writing and reading words

Student Grouping

- center
- small group
- independent

Materials

Each student will need the following:

- 1 copy of Word Roll and Write Sheet (1/2 of page 12)
- dice with words
- 1 pencil

Directions

Have each student do the following:

1. Roll a die and read the word.
2. Write that word in a box.
3. Choose a new die, roll it, read that word, and write that word in the next box.
4. Continue to roll and write until all of the boxes are filled in.

Helpful Hints

- Have extra copies available.
- Use wooden blocks to make word dice.
- Put different words on each die.

Word Roll and Write Sheet

Name _____

- -

Word Roll and Write Sheet

Name _____

Writing Lists

Literacy Skill
- writing words

Student Grouping
- center
- small group
- partner
- independent

Materials
Each student will need the following:
- 1 copy of School List, Animal List, Grocery List, or Wish List (1/2 of page 14, 23, 33 or 43)
- 1 pre-cut set of picture/word cards to match title of list: School Picture/Word Cards (pages 15–22), Animal Picture/Word Cards (pages 25–32), Grocery Picture/Word Cards (pages 35–42), or Wish Picture/Word Cards (pages 45–48)
- 1 pencil

Directions
Have each student do the following:
1. Place the picture/word cards of your chosen category (school, animal, grocery, or wish) in a pile.
2. Choose a picture/word card and read the word.
3. Write the word on your category list.
4. Continue choosing cards until the list is completed.

Helpful Hints
- Laminate picture cards for durability, especially if using in a literacy center.
- Have extra recording sheets available.
- Store each set in a separate small, plastic bag.
- Coordinate the writing lists with themes.

Name _____

School List

1. _____

2. _____

3. _____

4. _____

5. _____

6. _____

7. _____

8. _____

9. _____

10. _____

Name _____

School List

1. _____

2. _____

3. _____

4. _____

5. _____

6. _____

7. _____

8. _____

9. _____

10. _____

School Picture/Word Cards

bus

backpack

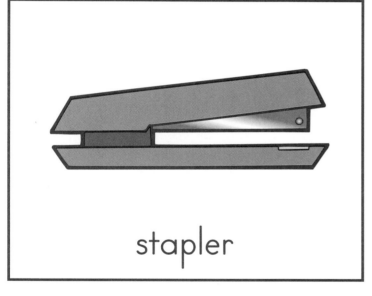

stapler

scissors

pencil

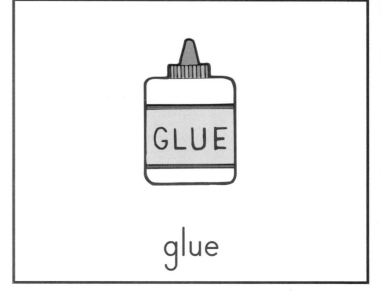

glue

School Picture/Word Cards

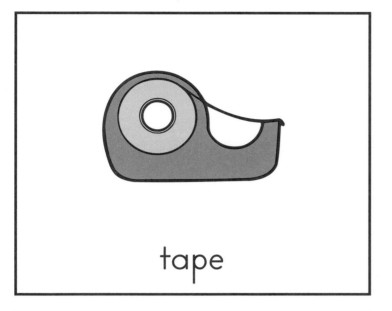

tape

book

teacher

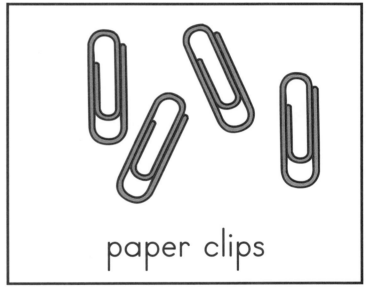

paper clips

crayons

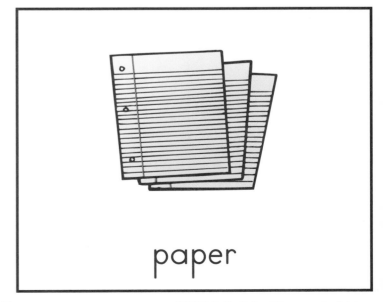

paper

School Picture/Word Cards

computer

table

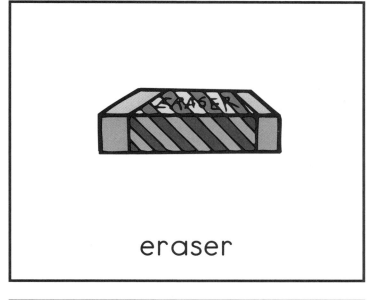

eraser

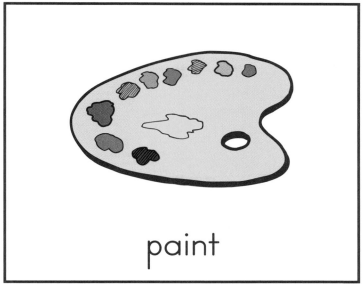

paint

chair

school

School Picture/Word Cards

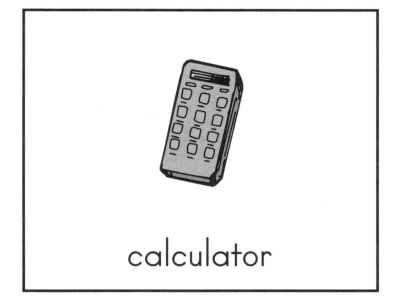

calculator

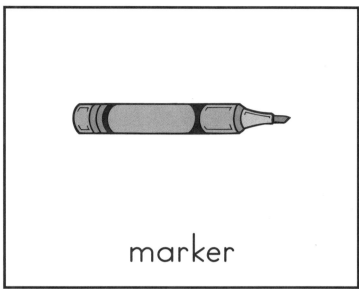

marker

calendar

globe

notebook

clock

22

Name _____

Animal List

1. _____

2. _____

3. _____

4. _____

5. _____

6. _____

7. _____

8. _____

9. _____

10. _____

Name _____

Animal List

1. _____

2. _____

3. _____

4. _____

5. _____

6. _____

7. _____

8. _____

9. _____

10. _____

24

Animal Picture/Word Cards

elephant

turtle

seal

tiger

lion

horse

Animal Picture/Word Cards

rabbit

frog

lizard

giraffe

mouse

bird

#3237 Full-Color Literacy Activities

Animal Picture/Word Cards

dolphin

alligator

zebra

monkey

fish

octopus

Animal Picture/Word Cards

cow

spider

snake

dog

bear

butterfly

Name _____

Grocery List

1. _____

2. _____

3. _____

4. _____

5. _____

6. _____

7. _____

8. _____

9. _____

10. _____

Name _____

Grocery List

1. _____

2. _____

3. _____

4. _____

5. _____

6. _____

7. _____

8. _____

9. _____

10. _____

Grocery Picture/Word Cards

bread

milk

juice

cookies

soda pop

apples

Grocery Picture/Word Cards

bananas

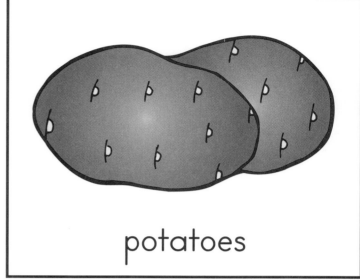

potatoes

jam

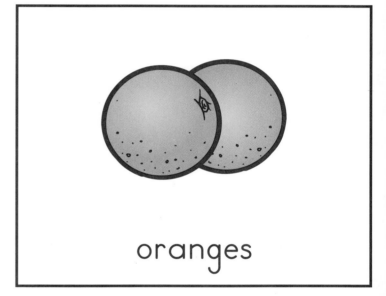

oranges

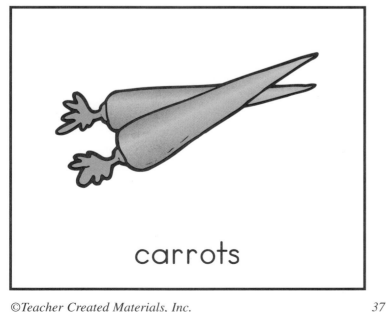

carrots

soup

38

Grocery Picture/Word Cards

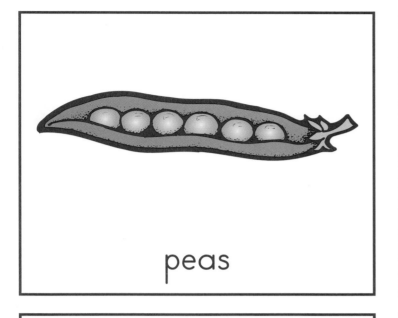

peas

chicken

cheese

cereal

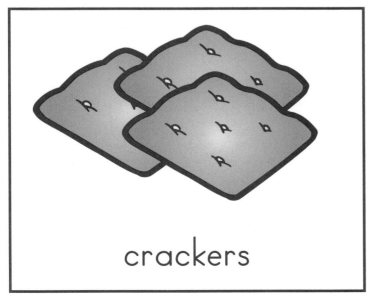

crackers

hot dogs

Grocery Picture/Word Cards

eggs

steak

ice cream

pickles

grapes

pizza

Name _____

Wish List

1. _____

2. _____

3. _____

4. _____

5. _____

6. _____

7. _____

8. _____

9. _____

10. _____

Name _____

Wish List

1. _____

2. _____

3. _____

4. _____

5. _____

6. _____

7. _____

8. _____

9. _____

10. _____

44

Wish Picture/Word Cards

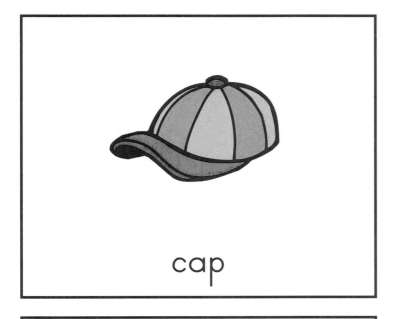

cap

book

ice skates

radio

top

bike

Wish Picture/Word Cards

dog

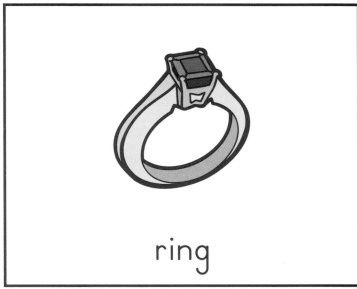

ring

sunglasses

watch

cat

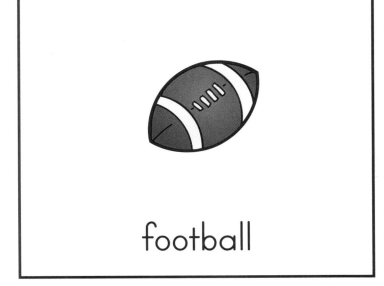

football

Write Around the Room

Literacy Skills

- writing words
- reading words

Student Grouping

- small group
- independent

Materials

Each student will need the following:

- 1 copy of Write Around the Room (1/2 of page 50)
- 1 clipboard
- 1 pencil

Directions

Have each student do the following:

1. Write 10 words of items that he or she sees around the room on his or her paper.
2. After their list is completed, have students read their lists to each other.

Helpful Hints

- Have extra copies available.
- This activity works best in a print-rich environment.

Name _____

Write Around the Room

1. _____

2. _____

3. _____

4. _____

5. _____

6. _____

7. _____

8. _____

9. _____

10. _____

Name _____

Write Around the Room

1. _____

2. _____

3. _____

4. _____

5. _____

6. _____

7. _____

8. _____

9. _____

10. _____

Shadow Writing

Literacy Skills
- writing sentences
- reading words

Student Grouping
- center
- small group
- independent

Materials
Each student will need the following:

- 1 copy of Shadow Writing (page 52, 53, 54, or 55)
- 1 pencil

Directions
Have each student do the following:

1. Read the sentence.
2. Use his or her best writing to write the sentence on the line below the printed sentence. (Use spacing, capital letters, punctuation, etc.)
3. Reread to check for accuracy.
4. Continue until all sentences have been neatly written.

Helpful Hints
- To make the activity more challenging, have the students independently write a sentence on the back of the paper.

I _____ see _____ the _____ owl.

I _____ like _____ skunks.

The _____ fox _____ is _____ red.

52

Shadow Writing (Weather)

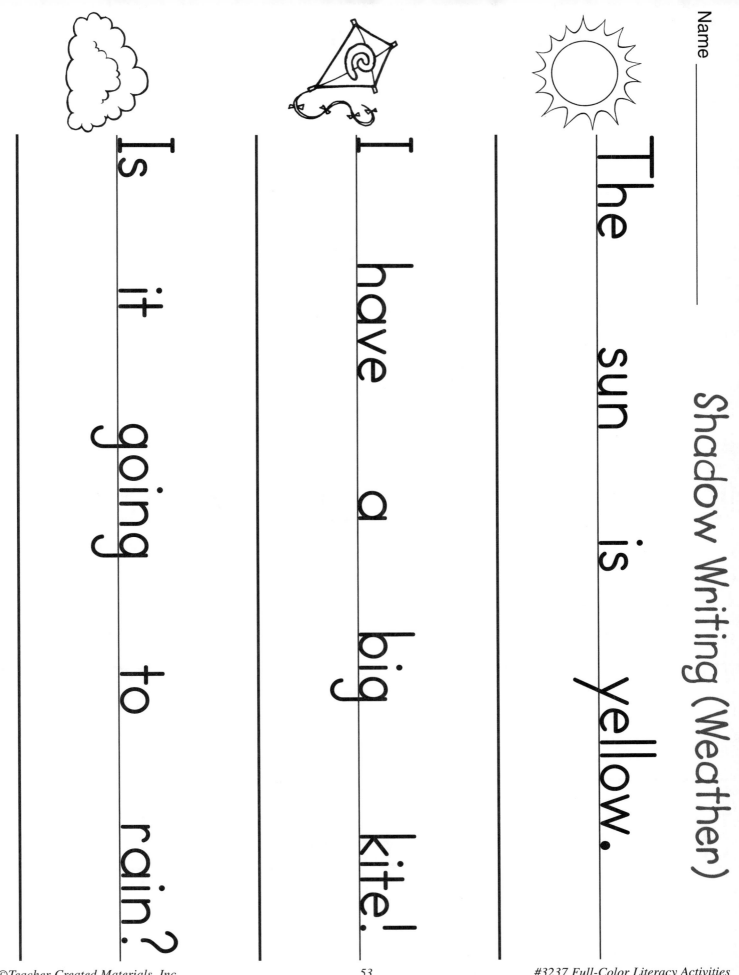

The sun is yellow.

I have a big kite!

Is it going to rain?

Shadow Writing (Winter)

Name _____

I see a snowman.

He has a hat.

It is snowing!

Shadow Writing (Hygiene)

Name _____

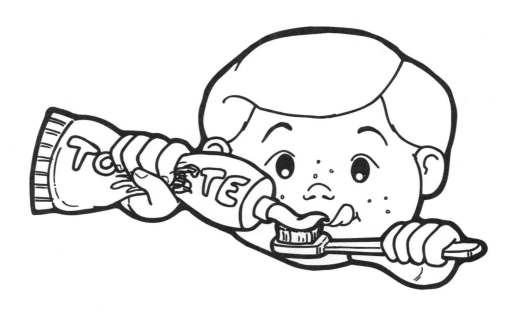

I brush my teeth.

I go to the dentist.

I lost a tooth!

Sentence Order

Literacy Skills

- writing words
- reading words
- reading comprehension

Student Grouping

- center
- small group
- independent

Materials

Each student will need the following:

- 1 copy of Sentence Order sheet (page 57 or 58)
- 1 pencil

Directions

Have each student do the following:

1. Look for the word that starts with a capital letter. Write that word on the first line under the sentence.
2. Read the rest of the words and write them in order. What would make sense/sound right?
3. Reread to check for accuracy.
4. Continue until all sentences have been placed in order.

Helpful Hint

- Remind students that all sentences start with a capital letter and that punctuation marks are used at the end of each sentence.

Sentence Order (Farm)

Name _____

Directions: The words below are out of order. Write the words in order to form sentences.

cow   at   Look   the

_____ _____ _____ _____ !

a   is   Here   pig

_____ _____ _____ _____ .

that   Is   sheep   a

_____ _____ _____ _____ ?

Sentence Order (Pets)

Name _____

Directions: The words below are out of order. Write the words in order to form sentences.

my   fish   Is   this

___ ___ ___ ___ ?

hop   can   The   frog

___ ___ ___ ___ .

is   The   turtle   big

___ ___ ___ ___ !

Write It!

Literacy Skill

- writing short vowel words

Student Grouping

- center
- partner
- small group
- independent

Materials

Each student will need the following:

- 1 copy of Write It! (1/2 of page 60)
- 1 pre-cut set of short vowel picture cards (pages 61 to 69)

Directions

Have each student do the following:

1. Lay out the picture cards.
2. Choose a picture card.
3. Say the name of the picture slowly.
4. Write the word on the line.
5. Continue until the sheet is complete.

Helpful Hints

- Have extra recording sheets available.
- Laminate cards for durability.
- Write the words on the back of the pictures so students can self-check.
- Concentrate on one vowel at a time.
- Have students try and read all the words on their sheets.

Name _____

Write It!

1. _____

2. _____

3. _____

4. _____

5. _____

6. _____

7. _____

8. _____

9. _____

10. _____

Name _____

Write It!

1. _____

2. _____

3. _____

4. _____

5. _____

6. _____

7. _____

8. _____

9. _____

10. _____

Short "a" Picture Cards

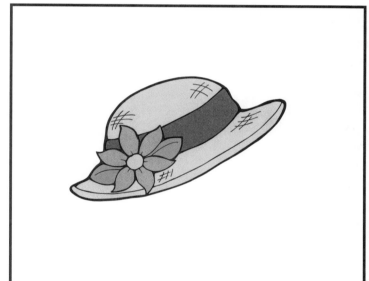

62

Short "e" Picture Cards

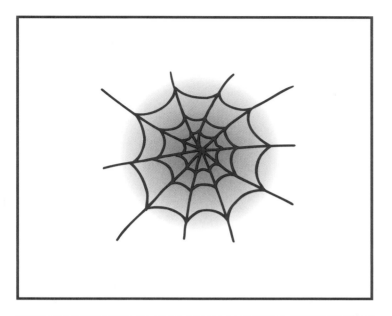

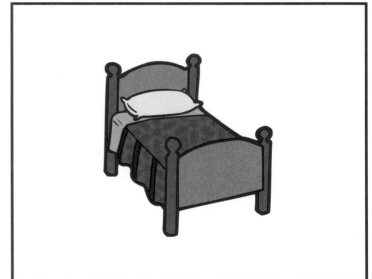

Short "i" Picture Cards

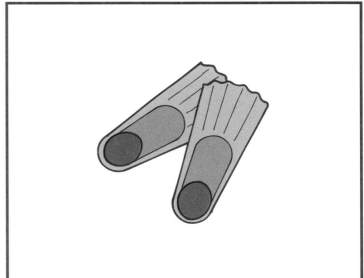

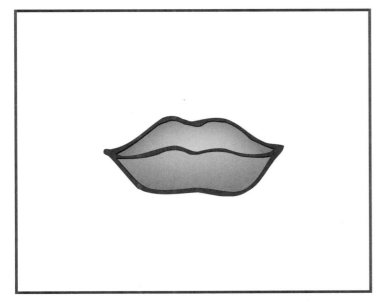

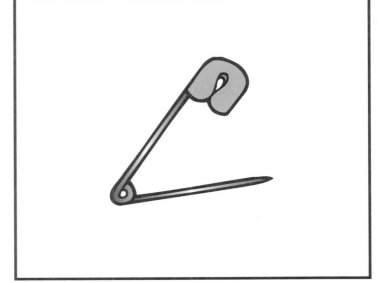

Short "o" Picture Cards

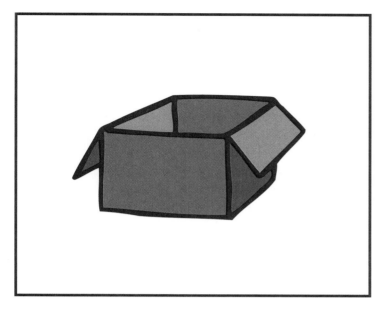

Short "u" Picture Cards

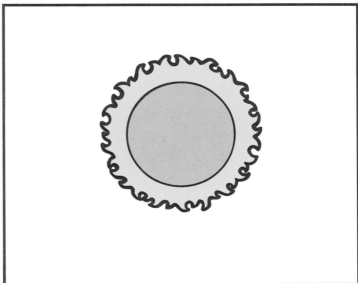

Today's News!

Literacy Skill
- writing

Student Grouping
- center
- whole group

Materials
Each student will need the following:

- 1 copy of Today's News! (page 72)
- 1 pencil

Directions
Have all students do the following:
1. Discuss the date and write it in the Today's Date box.
2. Discuss the weather and then draw a picture in the Today's Weather box.
3. Discuss any exciting classroom news that the students may want to share with their families (a party, field trip, class pet, etc.).
4. Decide what to write (Example: We have a new pet hamster. We named it Pepper.)
5. Watch the teacher write (discussing words, spacing, capital letters . . .).
6. Write the same message on his or her paper.
7. Take his or her Today's News! home to share with family.

Helpful Hint
- The teacher should model each step, stopping to make sure that all students are following along.

Today's News!

Today's Date: _____

Today's Weather

Nonfiction Report

Literacy Skill

- writing facts

Student Grouping

- center
- small group
- independent

Materials

Each student will need the following:

- 1 copy of My Report On _____ (page 74)
- nonfiction books about objects on which reports are to be written
- 1 pencil
- crayons

Directions

Have each student do the following:

1. Choose an object to write about (animal, insect, etc.).
2. Find a book that has information on that object.
3. Read or look through the book for interesting new facts.
4. Complete each sentence using the information from the book.
5. Draw a picture of the object being described in the space provided.

Helpful Hint

- Encourage your students to write new and interesting facts.

My Report On _____

They have _____.

They like to eat _____.

They live _____.

They like to _____.

74

Descriptive Writing

Literacy Skill

- descriptive writing

Student Grouping

- center
- small group
- independent

Materials

Each student will need the following:

- 1 copy of the descriptive writing sheet (page 76)
- 1 pencil
- crayons

Directions

Have each student do the following:

1. Choose an object to write about (animal, insect, person, etc.).
2. Write a descriptive title on the top of the page (Example: "The Very Silly Spider").
3. Complete each sentence trying to use descriptive words.
4. Draw a picture of the object being described in the space provided.

Helpful Hint

- This activity works well when doing an author study on Eric Carle (*The Very Hungry Caterpillar*, *The Very Quiet Cricket,* or *The Very Grouchy Ladybug*).

_____

am _____.

have _____.

like to _____.

But most of all . . .

_____.

Story Starters

Literacy Skill

- story writing

Student Grouping

- center
- independent

Materials

Each student will need the following:

- 1 pre-cut Story Starter Strip (pages 79 to 81)
- 1 pencil
- paper or writing journal

Directions

Have each student do the following:

1. Choose one Story Starter Strip.
2. Copy the words from the Story Starter Strip onto his or her paper.
3. Continue to write a story.

Helpful Hints

- Laminate the strips for durability.
- Have the story starters available at the writing center.

Story Starter Strips

I like _____ .

I see _____ .

I love _____ .

I can _____ .

What if _____ ?

At school _____ .

Once there was _____ .

If I had a _____ .

80

Story Starter Strips

I wonder _____ .

I wish I could _____ .

If I were a _____ .

Let me tell you about _____ .

One day _____ .

Long ago _____ .

Once upon a time _____ .

One dark night _____ .

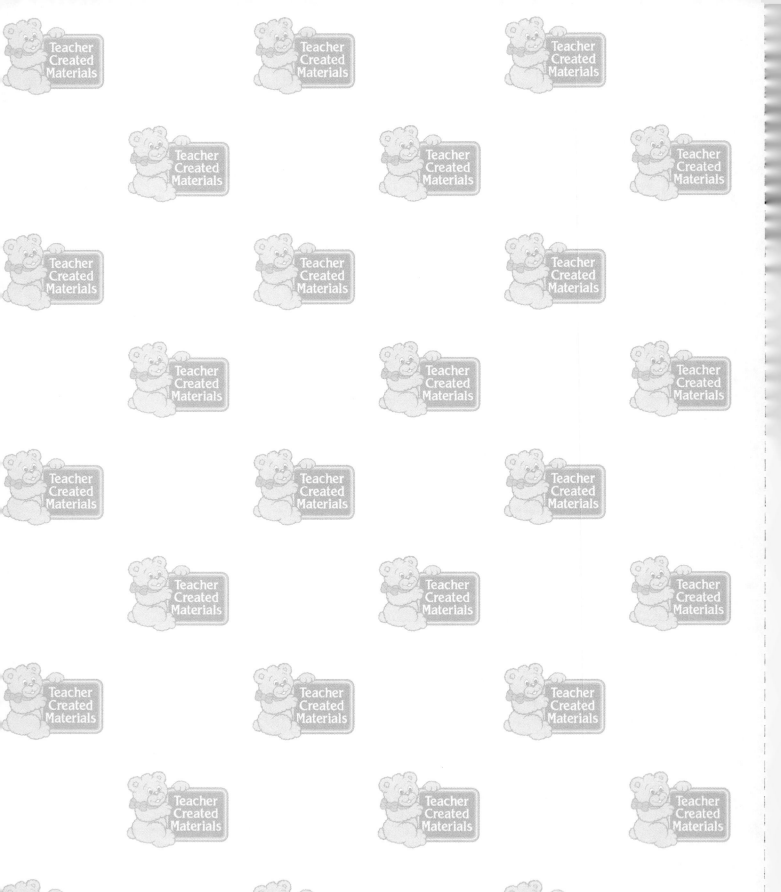

82

Write About It

Literacy Skill
- writing

Student Grouping
- center
- independent

Materials
Each student will need the following:

- 1 card from a pre-cut set of Topic Cards (pages 85 to 95)
- 1 pencil
- paper or writing journal

Directions
Have each student do the following:

1. Choose a topic card that interests him or her. (Example: baseball)
2. Write a story about the object on the card. (Example: I play baseball with my friends. We like to hit the ball.)

Helpful Hints
- These cards work great when students cannot think of anything to write about.
- Cut and laminate the cards for durability.
- Locate in an easily accessible area for students to use at any time.

84

Topic Cards

swimming

basketball

soccer

football

baseball

hockey

86

Topic Cards

sports

summer

spring

volcano

winter

fall

Topic Cards

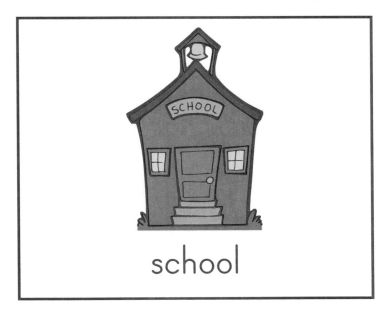

school

circus

car

money

clown

camping

Topic Cards

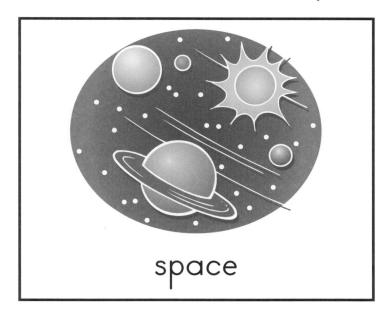

space

park

beach

aliens

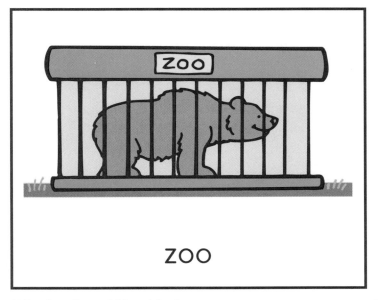

zoo

flowers

Topic Cards

birthday

farm

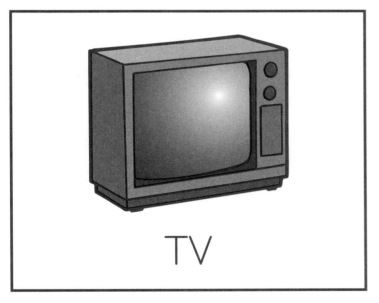

TV

family

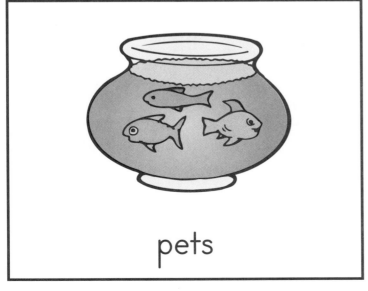

pets

computer

Topic Cards

dinosaur

garden

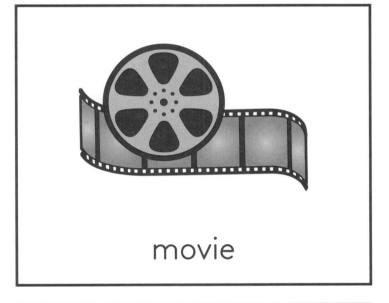

movie

ice cream

airplane

rainbow

Kids' Café
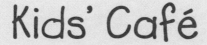

Literacy Skills

- reading a menu
- writing a food order
- writing a check

Student Grouping

- center
- small group
- partner

Materials

Each partner group will need the following:

- 1 copy of Kids' Café Menu (page 99 and 100)
- 2 copies of Kids' Café Ordering Tickets (page 101)
- 2 Checks (page 102) or play money
- play food (if available)
- 1 pencil

Directions

Have each partner group do the following:

1. Take turns ordering and paying for the food (customer) and writing the order and serving the food (waiter/waitress).

Helpful Hints

- Laminate the menu for durability.
- Run many copies of the above items to be used in a writing center.

98

Kids' Café Menu

Food

Hamburger	$4.00
Hotdog	$1.00
French Fries	$1.00
Pizza	$3.00
Soup	$2.00
Taco	$2.00

Desserts

 Popcorn $1.00

 Ice cream $2.00

 Cake $3.00

 Pie $3.00

Drinks

 Soda $1.00

 Milk $1.00

 Coffee $1.00

Kids' Café Ordering Tickets

Kids' Café

Thank you!   Total

Kids' Café

Thank you!   Total

Checks

Student _____ Date _____

To _____ $ [   ]

_____

_____

Student _____ Date _____

To _____ $ [   ]

_____

_____

Student _____ Date _____

To _____ $ [   ]

_____

_____

Create a Story

Literacy Skill
- writing

Student Grouping
- center
- independent

Materials
Students will need the following:
- several pre-cut copies of Create-a-Story Pictures (page 104)
- pre-made books (blank paper stapled together)
- glue
- pencils
- crayons

Directions
Have students do the following:
1. Have each student choose pictures that he or she will use to make his or her story. (The pictures are the illustrations. The students will write the words.)
2. Have each student lay out the pictures in order of his or her story.
3. Have each student draw a cover for his or her story.
4. Have each student glue the first picture onto the page after the cover. Have him or her write a sentence about the picture.
5. Continue this until all the pictures are placed on the pages of his or her book.

Helpful Hints
- It is important for students to think about their stories first before gluing them into their books.
- Put all pictures in a basket for students to use independently.
- Add different pictures in the basket each week.

Create-a-Story Pictures

  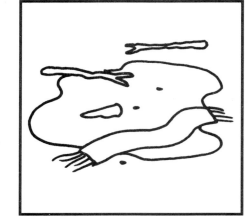

Die-namite Spelling

Literacy Skill
- writing sight words

Student Grouping
- center
- small group
- partner

Materials
Each group will need the following:
- 2 Die-namite Spelling writing sheets (1/2 of page 106)
- 2 Die-namite Spelling word lists (1/2 page 107, 109, or 111)
- 2 dice
- 1 pencil

Directions
Have each group do the following:
1. Each player rolls a die.
2. The player who rolls the highest number gets to write word #1.
3. Players roll dice again.
4. The player who rolls the highest number writes the next word on his or her list. If the same player wins again, he or she would write word #2. If the other player wins, he or she writes word #1.
5. Continue until someone has all 10 words written. The other player(s) should write the rest of his or her words before ending the game.

Helpful Hints
- Laminate the word lists.
- Have extra writing sheets available.
- Choose a word list that is appropriate for each student group.

Name _____

Die-namite Spelling!

1. _____

2. _____

3. _____

4. _____

5. _____

6. _____

7. _____

8. _____

9. _____

10. _____

Name _____

Die-namite Spelling!

1. _____

2. _____

3. _____

4. _____

5. _____

6. _____

7. _____

8. _____

9. _____

10. _____

Name _____ | Name _____

Die-namite Spelling!   # Die-namite Spelling!

1.   I   1.   I

2.   like   2.   like

3.   my   3.   my

4.   see   4.   see

5.   love   5.   love

6.   a   6.   a

7.   the   7.   the

8.   mom   8.   mom

9.   cat   9.   cat

10. dad   10. dad

Name _____

Die-namite Spelling!

1. love

2. go

3. can

4. me

5. and

6. is

7. we

8. dog

9. look

10. at

Name _____

Die-namite Spelling!

1. love

2. go

3. can

4. me

5. and

6. is

7. we

8. dog

9. look

10. at

Name _____

Die-namite Spelling!

1. you
2. that
3. he
4. she
5. it
6. have
7. not
8. come
9. will
10. here

Name _____

Die-namite Spelling!

1. you
2. that
3. he
4. she
5. it
6. have
7. not
8. come
9. will
10. here

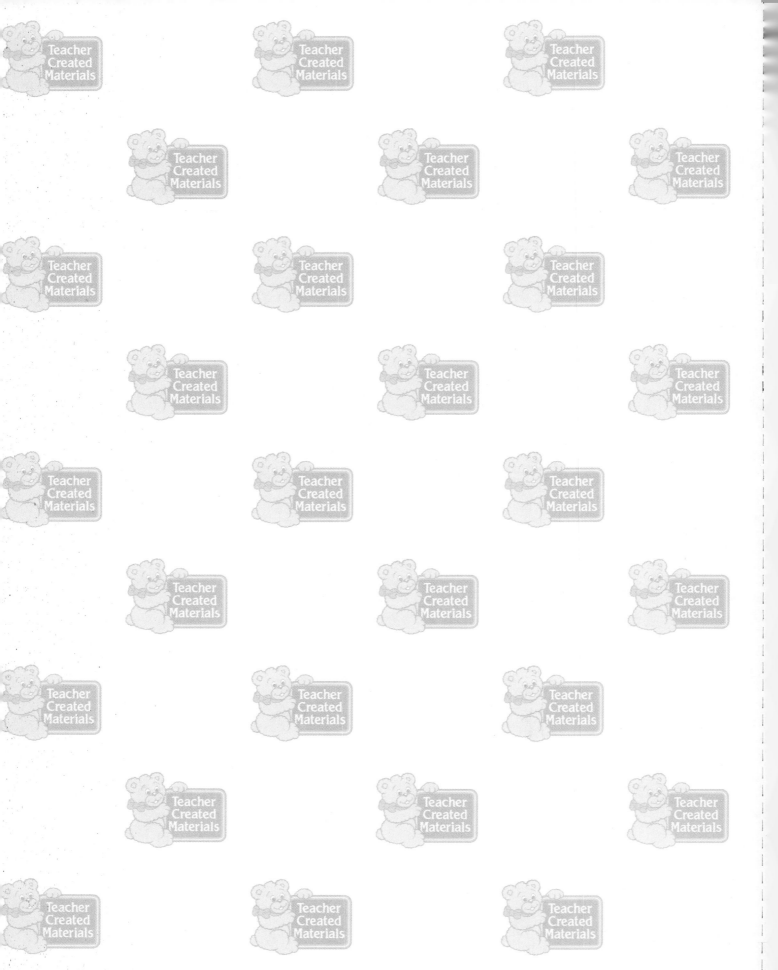

Fix It!

Literacy Skills

- reading words
- writing words
- editing

Student Grouping

- center
- small group
- independent

Materials

Each student will need the following:

- 1 copy of Fix-It! Sentences (page 114, 115, or 116)
- paper
- 1 pencil

Directions

Have each student do the following:

1. Read the first sentence. The number at the end of each sentence tells how many mistakes he or she must find.
2. Write the first sentence "fixing" the mistakes on the line. Check for spacing, capital letters, punctuation, and correct spelling. For example, "Look at thepig" (2 mistakes) would be rewritten as "Look at the pig!" on the lines.
3. Continue "fixing" the rest of the sentences, and reread to check for accuracy.

Helpful Hint

- Review when to use capital letters, spacing, and punctuation marks.

Fix-It! Sentences

i love my dad.

Do you like me?

I can see tHe cat.

114

Name: ______________________

Fix-It! Sentences

go andget the toy. (2)

____

I liketo read (2)

____

Look at thepig (2)

____

Name: ______________________

Fix-It! Sentences

Canyou see sam

3

teh dog is Big!

3

Thezoo si fun

3

Pull a Sentence

Literacy Skills

- sentence writing
- reading words

Student Grouping

- center
- independent

Materials

Each student will need the following:

- pre-cut Pull-a-Sentence Strips (pages 119 and 121) to place in a bag or basket
- 1 pencil
- paper or writing journal

Directions

Have each student do the following:

1. Choose a sentence strip from the bag or basket.
2. Copy the sentence onto his or her paper.
3. Complete the sentence.
4. Read the sentence to a friend.

Helpful Hints

- Laminate the strips for durability.
- Have the sentence strips available at the writing center.

Pull-a-Sentence Strips

I like to _____ .

I can see _____ .

I love my _____ .

I wish I were a _____ .

I like to eat _____ .

I play with my _____ .

I have a _____ .

This is a big _____ !

Pull-a-Sentence Strips

Look at the _____ !

Can you see my _____ ?

Here is a red _____ .

Yes, I love to _____ !

The cat is _____ .

I went to the _____ .

Come and see my _____ .

Is it in the _____ ?

Select Your Own

Literacy Skill

- writing

Student Grouping

- center
- small group
- independent

Materials

Each student will need the following:

- 1 copy of stationery (page 128, 129, 130, 131, or 132)
- 1 pencil

Directions

Have each student do the following:

1. Use the stationery to write lists, words, sentences, or stories.

Helpful Hint

- Have extra sheets available in a writing center.

128

Independent Writing Books

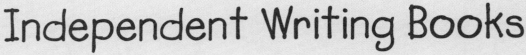

Literacy Skill

- writing

Student Grouping

- center
- independent

Materials

Each student will need the following:

- 1 copy of a pre-made book cover (page 134, 135, or 136)
- blank paper
- 1 pencil
- crayons

Directions

Have each student do the following:

1. Choose one of the pre-made covers and one blank page.
2. Color the cover.
3. On the blank page, have students do the following based on the cover they chose: I Love Books!—Draw a picture of your favorite book and write a sentence why it is your favorite; I Lost a Tooth!—Write a sentence and draw a picture about losing a tooth; Ouch!—Write a sentence and draw a picture of a time when he or she got hurt.

Helpful Hints

- Bind several pieces of paper to each cover to create a larger book.
- Put these books in an area of the room where they can easily be reached. Students will then be able to read their books to their friends or add to the books.

I Love Books!

By

_____

Ouch!

By

_____

I Lost
a
Tooth!

By

_____

Reading
Activities

Missing Word

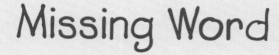

Literacy Skills
- reading words
- reading comprehension

Student Grouping
- center
- small group
- partner
- independent

Materials

Each student will need the following:

- 1 set of Missing Word Sentences (page 139 or 141)
- 1 pre-cut set of Missing Word Cards (1/2 of page 143)

Directions

Have each student do the following:

1. Read the first sentence.
2. Read all of the word cards.
3. Decide which word would best complete the sentence.
4. Continue until all words have been used.
5. Read all four sentences again. Do they all make sense? Do they sound right?

Helpful Hints
- Laminate the mats and cards for durability.
- Store cards in small, plastic bags.

Missing Word Sentences (Set A)

Do you love my _____ ? .

Can you run _____ ? .

What do you like to _____ ? .

Is it in the _____ ? .

Missing Word Sentences (Set B)

I wish I had a _____ .

I see the yellow _____ .

I like to _____ .

I like to eat _____ .

Missing Word Cards (Set A)

box	do
fast	car

Missing Word Cards (Set B)

apples	dog
play	sun

144

Mystery Objects

Literacy Skills

- reading words
- reading comprehension

Student Grouping

- center
- small group
- partner
- independent

Materials

Each student will need the following:

- Mystery Objects Riddle Cards pre-cut (pages 147 and 149)
- Mystery Objects Picture Cards pre-cut (pages 151 and 153)

Directions

Have each student do the following:

1. Place all the Mystery Objects Picture Cards face up on a flat surface.
2. Place the Mystery Objects Riddle Cards in a pile.
3. Choose a riddle card and read the sentences.
4. Look at the pictures and decide which would best answer "What am I?"
5. Continue until all the riddles have been solved.

Helpful Hints

- Laminate all the cards for durability, especially if using the activity in a center.
- Store the cards in small, plastic bags.

146

Mystery Object Riddle Cards

What am I?

I like to hop.

I love to eat carrots.

I have big ears.

What am I?

I am green.

I like to eat flies.

I love to jump.

What am I?

I am at the zoo.

I eat yellow bananas.

I have a long tail.

What am I?

I have a long neck.

I have brown spots.

I eat leaves.

What am I?

I am black.

I come out at night.

I have wings.

What am I?

I lay eggs in a nest.

I live on a farm.

I have feathers.

Mystery Object Riddle Cards

What am I?

I have a shell.

I am green.

I am slow.

What am I?

I am black.

I like to eat insects.

I have eight legs.

What am I?

I am red.

I grow on trees.

I am a fruit.

What am I?

I have fins.

I live in water.

I like to swim.

What am I?

I like cheese.

I do not like cats.

I can run fast.

What am I?

I am pink.

I like mud.

I live in a barn.

Mystery Object Picture Cards

rabbit

frog

monkey

giraffe

bat

chicken

Mystery Object Picture Cards

spider

turtle

fish

apple

pig

mouse

154

Mixed-up Sentences

Literacy Skills
- reading words
- reading comprehension

Student Grouping
- center
- small group
- partner
- independent

Materials
Each student will need the following:
- 1 pre-cut copy of Mixed-up Sentence Cards (page 157, 159, 161, 163, 165, or 167)

Directions
Have each student do the following:
1. Look for the word card that starts with a capital letter. Put that at the beginning of the sentence.
2. Look for the punctuation mark card. Put that at the end of the sentence.
3. Read the rest of the word cards and put them in order. What would make sense or sound right?
4. Reread to check for accuracy.
5. Continue until all sentences have been unscrambled.

Helpful Hints
- Laminate the cards for durability, especially if using them in a center.
- Store activity sets in small, plastic bags.
- Read the sentence to the child first and then scramble it.
- Review the concept that all sentences start with a capital letter and end with a punctuation mark.

Mixed-up Sentence Cards

I like to play at the park.

I

like

to

play

at

the

park

.

Mixed-up Sentence Cards

My mom is in the house.

My

mom

is

in

the

house

.

160

Mixed-up Sentence Cards

Do you have a brown dog?

Do

you

have

a

brown

dog

?

Mixed-up Sentence Cards

Can you see my big snowman?

Can

you

see

my

big

snowman

?

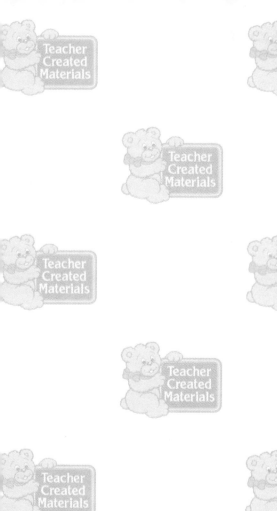

Mixed-up Sentence Cards

Look at the red apple in this tree!

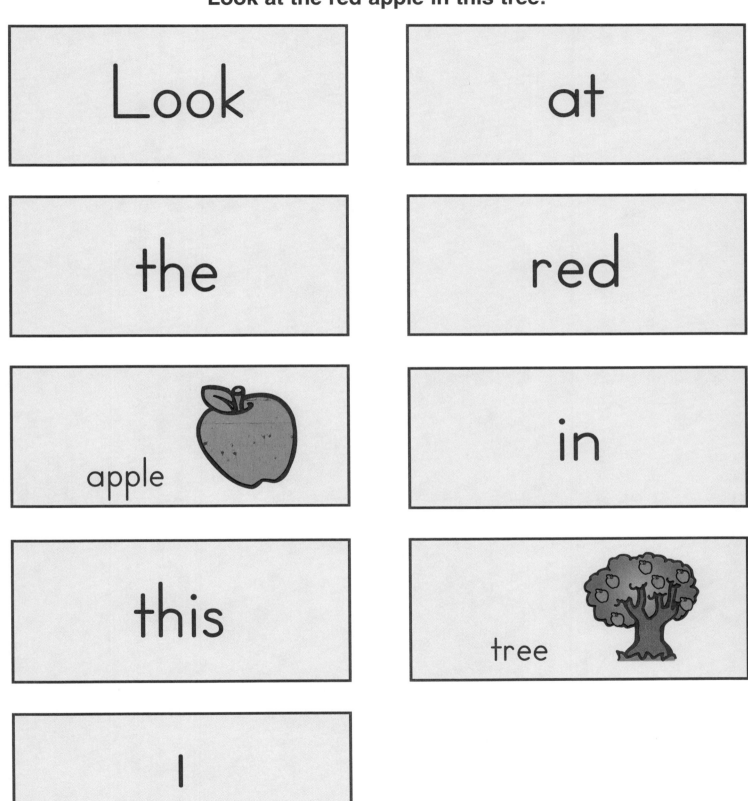

Look

at

the

red

apple

in

this

tree

!

Mixed-up Sentence Cards

I love to go to my school!

I	love
to	go
to	my
school	!

Scrambled Sentences

Literacy Skills
- reading words
- reading comprehension

Student Grouping
- center
- small group
- independent

Materials
Each student will need the following:

- 1 copy of Scrambled Sentence Strips sheet (page 170, 171, or 172)
- 1 piece of paper
- scissors
- glue
- crayons

Directions
Have each student do the following:

1. Choose a sentence strip from the sheet and read it.
2. Cut the sentence out. Then cut it apart word by word and scramble the words.
3. Look for the word that starts with a capital letter which will be the beginning of the sentence.
4. Look for the punctuation mark that will be at the end of the sentence.
5. Read the rest of the words and put them in order. What would make sense or sound right?
6. Reread to check for accuracy.
7. Glue the words of the sentence on the paper in the correct order. Remember to space the words.
8. Draw a picture to go with the sentence.
9. Choose another sentence strip from the sheet and repeat the process again.

Helpful Hints
- Check each student's work before he or she glues.
- Make sure the student is working on one sentence at a time.

Scrambled Sentence Strips (Fall)

I see a big pumpkin .

The bat is black .

I like red apples .

I see the spider !

The owl is in a tree .

Scrambled Sentence Strips (Winter)

Playing | in | the | snow | is | fun | !

The | snow | is | white | .

Look | at | the | snow | on | my | hat | .

Can | you | see | my | snowman | ?

I | see | a | big | snowman | !

I | love | to | play | in | the | snow | .

Scrambled Sentence Strips (Spring)

The kite is up in the sky .

The baby bird is in a nest .

Look at the big rainbow !

I can see a brown bunny .

I love to play in the rain !

Here comes the big sun !

Stamp a Story

Literacy Skills
- reading words
- reading comprehension

Student Grouping
- center
- small group
- partner

Materials
Each student will need the following:
- 1 copy of a Stamp-a-Story sheet (page 174, 175, or 176)
- picture stamps
- 1 ink pad

Directions
Have each student do the following:
1. Find a stamp of an animal (for example, a cat). This will be what the story is about. Stamp the animal on the title line.
2. Read the first sentence. Use the same animal stamp to fill in the blank.
3. Read the second sentence and find another stamp that fits in that sentence blank. What would make sense or sound right?
4. Continue until each line has a stamp on it.
5. Read the story. Does it make sense?

Helpful Hints
- Encourage students to think about the sentence before stamping in the blanks.
- Have white correction tape available to cover up mistakes. Students will be able to stamp right over it.
- If picture stamps are not available, students can write the word on the line.

The _____

This is my _____ . It is in a _____ .

My _____ likes _____ . It eats _____ and

_____ . My _____ likes to go to the _____ .

It likes red _____ and blue _____ . Did

you see my _____ ?